A GIFT FOR

FROM

DEDICATION

TO OUR GOOD FRIENDS

GEORGE AND ARLYS OSBORN.

MAY YOUR PILLOW TALK

BE AS SWEET AS THE SCONES

YOU SO OFTEN LEAVE AT OUR FRONT DOOR.

pillow talk
for couples

drawing closer
before the
lights go out

drs. *les & leslie* parrott

J COUNTRYMAN®

NASHVILLE, TENNESSEE
WWW.JCOUNTRYMAN.COM

Published by J. Countryman®, a division of Thomas Nelson, Inc.,

Nashville, Tennessee 37214

Design by Koechel Peterson and Associates, Inc., Minneapolis, Minnesota

Photography by Tom Henry, Koechel Peterson and Associates, Inc.

ISBN 0-8499-9662-7

Printed and bound in Belgium

www.thomasnelson.com

www.jcountryman.com

Making Your Heavenly Bed

An Introduction

We'd started from Seattle early in the morning and hassled with delayed connections in Denver when our plane finally touched down at the airport in Dallas. It was well after midnight and we were booked for an early morning television interview, followed by speaking engagements. We were weary to the bone when we drove up to the hotel entrance, where the bellhop unloaded our luggage and pointed us toward the front desk as the valet parked our rental car.

"This is nice," Leslie said as she gave the lobby the once over.

"It's great, I just hope the bed is as nice as the lobby," I quipped.

"We don't think you'll be disappointed," the clerk at the registration desk commented. "You'll be sleeping in a 'heavenly bed' tonight—it's our trademark."

At first I thought she was joking, but then she pointed to a sign on the desk describing the care and quality the hotel puts into their beds. As Brian, the bellhop, showed us the way to the elevator and then to our room, he also commented on how great the hotel beds were. *What a bunch of hype*, I thought to myself. *What can they do to a bed?*

"Your thermostat is to your left and your television remote is on the set," Brian said as he held open the door to our room. "And of course, this is your heavenly bed with 600-count sheets and a goose-down comforter."

I had to admit, it didn't look like your ordinary hotel bed. It was big, white, feathery, and fluffy. It was everything my weary body wanted.

"Sweet dreams," Brian said as he closed our hotel door.

We wasted no time climbing into the luxurious bed and we were quickly off to sleep. Our wake-up call came early the next morning. But as we were getting ready for our busy day, I commented to Leslie, "That may have been a short night, but I feel pretty rested."

She agreed. The bed was, well, "heavenly."

That night of divine sleep got us to thinking about our own bed at home. Shortly after flying back to Seattle we made a trip to a linen store where we purchased a big, white, fluffy down comforter, a thick mattress cover, feathery pillows, and some high-quality sheets. We wanted to create our own "heavenly bed." And we did. Because, on average, we humans spend about a third of our lives in bed, we decided it was worth the investment.

Truth be told, however, the perfect bed is not simply about sheets and pillows. It's about the relationship of the husband and wife who sleep

The perfect bed is not simply about sheets and pillows. It's about the relationship of the husband and wife who sleep on them.

As you give more attention to the minutes you have at your day's end, you will not only wake up more refreshed, but your relationship will be more alive.

on them. It's about the tone they set in the late night hours as they are dozing off to sleep, side-by-side. More important than the quality of the linens is the quality of the relationship. And the time we spend as a couple in bed talking about the residue of the day and our plans for tomorrow—our pillow talk—becomes some of the most important and precious moments in marriage.

And that is why we dedicate this little book to helping you make your pillow talk the best it can be. In the pages that follow, you will find meditations, quips, quotes, and discussion starters to help you both enjoy sweet slumber. As you give more attention to the minutes you have at your day's end, you will not only wake up more refreshed, but your relationship will be more alive. So take a few minutes—beginning tonight—to create your own "heavenly bed." It's worth the investment, and more.

Les and Leslie Parrott
Seattle, Washington

Before the Lights Go Out

THE MOST IMPORTANT MINUTES OF YOUR MARRIAGE CAN BE THE ONES YOU SPEND TOGETHER JUST before you fall asleep, but far too many couples waste this precious opportunity. They don't give it a second thought. They doze off to late-night chatter on the television, a book that makes them drowsy, or maybe the sound of a machine that blocks out distractions. Of course, there's nothing wrong with any of these things, but these couples are missing out on one of their best opportunities to make a meaningful connection. They are ending their day stuck in a rut of simply falling asleep in the same bed.

Even more separate at night are the couples who go to bed at different times—one's a night owl and the other an early riser. And then there are couples where one spouse works a night shift and isn't even home when the other goes to bed.

By picking up this book, we know you want something better. We know you recognize the value of

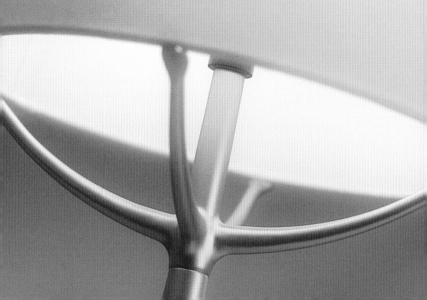

Your relationship will be rewarded abundantly because of the few minutes you invest in it at the close of your day. You will sleep more soundly, diminish needless quarrels, and feel more in tune with each other.

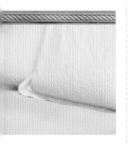

Find your own style of using these meditations, and as you do, the two of you will dream sweet dreams and become more deeply connected than ever before.

drawing closer to each other before the lights go out. As you cultivate this ritual, we can tell you from surveying hundreds of other couples and from our own personal experience, that your relationship will be rewarded abundantly because of the few minutes you invest in it at the close of your day. You will sleep more soundly, diminish needless quarrels, and feel more in tune with each other. Not to mention that your immune system will be built up and your waking hours more productive.

So make a pact. Try an experiment. Use the twenty-five meditations in this little book to draw closer together each night. If you go to bed at different times, that's okay. When one of you is ready for bed, simply take five or ten minutes together in your bed to connect with one of these meditations. Then the night owl can tuck the other partner in before moving on to another activity. Couples on alternative work schedules might need to adapt even more. The point is, you can find your own style of using these meditations, and as you do, the two of you will dream sweet dreams and become more deeply connected than ever before. We know of few investments that pay such big dividends.

Before You Fall Asleep

What would help each of you to read this book together well? Talk about your differing sleep styles and how you can best incorporate this new ritual of a nightly connection into your day's end. After a few times of doing this it will become a habit you'll look forward to each night.

A Verse to Sleep On

TWO ARE BETTER THAN ONE, BECAUSE THEY HAVE A GOOD REWARD FOR THEIR LABOR. FOR IF THEY FALL, ONE WILL LIFT UP HIS COMPANION. BUT WOE TO HIM WHO IS ALONE WHEN HE FALLS, FOR HE HAS NO ONE TO HELP HIM UP. AGAIN, IF TWO LIE DOWN TOGETHER, THEY WILL KEEP WARM; BUT HOW CAN ONE BE WARM ALONE? (ECCLESIASTES 4:9–11)

A Good Night Prayer

Lord, as we begin cultivating this nightly habit of "pillow talk" help us draw closer to each other as husband and wife. But we also ask that as we do this You will help us draw closer to You. We confess our need of You and know that whatever goodness we enjoy is because of Your grace. Thank You. Amen. ☾

Make sure you never, never argue at night.
You just lose a good night's sleep, and you
can't settle anything until morning anyway.

ROSE FITZGERALD KENNEDY

A Different Kind of Shut-Eye

MARTIN LUTHER, WHOSE QUESTIONING OF CHURCH PRACTICES LED TO THE PROTESTANT REFORMATION, JUST AS EASILY COULD HAVE BEGUN A MOVEMENT IN MODERN-DAY MARRIAGES WITH THIS QUOTE:

"It is impossible to keep peace between man and woman in family life if they do not condone and overlook each other's faults but watch everything to the smallest point. For who does not at times offend?"

It's difficult to improve on that point. Can you imagine what would happen in your home if both of you suddenly began overlooking petty problems? What would happen if you both decided to bypass opportunities to criticize? What would happen if suddenly, tomorrow this occurred in every home? It would be nothing short of a revolution.

Love must be blind if it is to grow. For as Luther said, "Who does not at times offend?" We all have

Love must be blind if it is to grow.

supplied plenty of opportunities for our spouse to find fault. That goes with the territory. The trick is learning how to shut our eyes to each other's faults.

Here are a couple of suggestions:

First, focus on what you like. In one of our university classes, we sometimes tell our students to take ten seconds to notice everything in the room that's green. Suddenly, they see it everywhere. Why? Because they're in a green mindset. That's all they were looking for. The same is true in marriage. When we invoke a positive mindset for our partner, all we begin to see is everything they do that is good, not bad.

Second, own up to your own faults. How would you like to be married to you? What about you would make you a challenge to live with? The more you recognize the difficulties you bring to the table, the more you will be able to accept your partner's.

Before You Fall Asleep

Talk to each other about what you think it would be like to be married to you. What would be good and what would be a challenge? Be as honest and as specific as you can, but be gentle with one another—this is pillow talk, not a pillow fight.

A Verse to Sleep On

(LOVE) IS NOT RUDE, IT IS NOT SELF-SEEKING, IT IS NOT EASILY ANGERED, IT KEEPS NO RECORD OF WRONGS (I CORINTHIANS 13:5, NIV).

A Good Night Prayer

God, tonight we ask You to help us with something we could never do on our own. We need Your help to empty ourselves of our compulsive need to correct each other. Fill us with more of You so that we might offer each other the kind of grace You give us. Amen. ℂ

There is a time for many words, and there is also a time for sleep.

Homer

Clean Sheets for a Fresh Start

WHEN I (LES) WAS WORKING ON MY DOCTORAL DISSERTATION, I WAS IMMERSED IN HEADY STUDIES ON GUILT AND REMORSE. I spent countless hours in the library researching the subject, and one of the research librarians came to know me and my topic well. Most days the librarian would stop by with a few more articles or research leads for me. On one occasion, however, she dropped off a paper with a note saying, "Thought this was funny." The page contained this little story: A shoplifter writes to a department store and says, "I've just become a Christian, and I can't sleep at night because I feel guilty. So here's $100 that I owe you." The "former" shoplifter signed his name, and in a little postscript at the bottom added, "If I still can't sleep, I'll send you the rest."

Few things prohibit a good night's sleep more than a nagging conscience. Who among us hasn't tossed and turned into the wee hours because of remorse about saying an unkind word or behaving more selfishly than usual? Guilt has robbed countless couples of a good night's rest. But it doesn't have to. There is a simple remedy to this late night torment, and it involves making a clean start.

Tonight, as you are getting tucked in, consider anything that might be nagging your conscience. Maybe it was the way you brushed off your spouse's request for a favor earlier in the week. Maybe you barked an order when you were under pressure. Perhaps it was a critical attitude or a snide remark you regret saying. Most of us have little difficulty recalling something we later regretted having said or done. Whatever might be tugging at your conscience, why don't the two of you go to bed tonight with clean sheets, with a fresh start. How? Saying a simple "I'm sorry" may be the ticket. A good old-fashioned apology may be just what the doctor ordered for allaying anything that's pestering your principles. A clean confession accompanied by heart-felt sorrow can give both of you the best night's sleep you've had in months.

Before You Fall Asleep

Can you recall a time, maybe from your childhood, when you didn't apologize for something you felt badly for? What did it do to your insides? And can you recall a time when you came clean on something that gave you a fresh start? Discuss the experience.

A Verse to Sleep On

I ACKNOWLEDGED MY SIN TO YOU, AND MY INIQUITY I HAVE NOT HIDDEN. I SAID, I WILL CONFESS MY TRANSGRESSIONS TO THE LORD, AND YOU FORGAVE THE INIQUITY OF MY SIN (PSALM 32:5).

A Good Night Prayer

Lord, too many times we say or do something that we know we shouldn't. And then we try to ignore it, hoping it will just go away. But You built within us a conscience that often reminds us to do the right thing. Thank You for this little alarm system. Help us, as a couple, to pay close attention to it as we interact with each other in the coming days. Amen. ☾

Those who dream by day are cognizant of many things
which escape those who dream only by night.

EDGAR ALLAN POE

Dream a Dream & Clear Your Mind

"Copy ... sheets ... copy."

"What?" I asked Leslie, who was obviously dreaming, as we lay in bed.

"The sheets must be copied, please," she replied sternly with eyes still closed as she tossed and turned.

"You're dreaming," I said softly.

Her eyes flashed open and she looked around the room for a moment. "What a weird dream."

"You were probably dreaming about getting a copy of our manuscript made," I suggested.

"No," Leslie said, still rubbing the sleep from her eyes.

"I dreamed you had painted a beautiful scene on our bedroom sheets and I wanted copies made so we wouldn't lose it."

Strange, indeed. Especially since I don't paint—on sheets or anything else.

Dreams, those mystical fantasies of slumber, are often bizarre and we can't always make much sense of them. But everybody dreams. A normal night's sleep always includes not one, but several periods of dreaming. This has been established by research studies beyond any doubt. The question for years has been *what do these dreams do?* Today's experts are finding answers. During dream sleep, the brain consolidates memory, clears our unresolved issues, and helps us forget things we don't need to remember. It is like the hard drive

on your computer that needs cleaning up from time to time. That is what dream sleep does for the mind.

So here's the key to a good night's dream: You have to get enough dream sleep to achieve the benefits. If you only sleep for six hours, you will be missing out on several major periods of dreaming and will not be getting enough dream sleep. So do what you can, together, to get the sleep you need, not just for your body, but for your mind, too.

Before You Fall Asleep

Explore what you might learn from your dreams tonight. Decide to remember what you dream. Sounds funny, but it has been shown experimentally that simply being motivated to recall your dreams really does improve your powers of recall. It also helps to have a note pad and pen by your bedside to write down what you dreamed.

A Verse to Sleep On

I WILL POUR OUT OF MY SPIRIT ON ALL FLESH; YOUR SONS AND YOUR DAUGHTERS SHALL PROPHESY, YOUR YOUNG MEN SHALL SEE VISIONS, YOUR OLD MEN SHALL DREAM DREAMS (ACTS 2:17).

A Good Night Prayer

Lord, You created us with the capacity to dream. Thank You for this gift that cleans up the "hard drive" of our mind. And as we pay particular attention to it tonight, show us what You might want us to see. Speak to us through our dreams and rejuvenate our minds as we rest. Amen. ℭ

In the Morning

What did you dream? Do you think God told you anything while you slept?

HUSBAND

WIFE

During dream sleep, the brain consolidates memory, clears our unresolved issues, and helps us forget things we don't need to remember.

Under Cover Touching

TIMMY WAS TERRIFIED OF THUNDERSTORMS. HIS MOM AND DAD WOULD SAY, "NOW, TIMMY, DON'T BE AFRAID. GOD IS RIGHT HERE IN THE ROOM WITH YOU." He would agree, but then as mommy and daddy went into their room, the lightning flashed, the thunder rolled, and Timmy screamed bloody murder. Timmy's daddy and mommy went back into his room: "Honey, we thought we told you, you don't need to be afraid. God is right here in the room with you."

"I know God is right here in the room with me," Timmy responds, "but I need someone with skin on."

It's easy to identify with this kid. We all want someone with skin on, and that's one of the great blessings of going to bed as a married couple. The holding, cuddling, and spooning we enjoy as husband and wife is wonderful. You know the feeling of holding each other tight under the covers during a storm. You know the comfort of warming each other's bodies as you climb into bed on a crisp autumn evening. You know the feeling of a gentle caress after a tough day

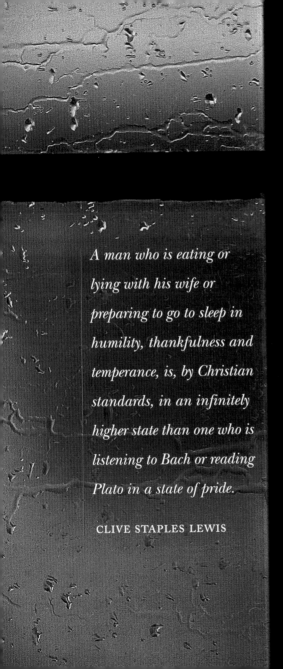

A man who is eating or lying with his wife or preparing to go to sleep in humility, thankfulness and temperance, is, by Christian standards, in an infinitely higher state than one who is listening to Bach or reading Plato in a state of pride.

CLIVE STAPLES LEWIS

or holding hands across the bed as you fall asleep on a summer's eve. Sometimes just the touch of a toe (even if it's cold) to be assured of your partner's presence is all it takes. Whatever its form, touch—that gentle, warm, magnificent gift—is glorious.

Touch can happen at any point throughout the night. Sometimes at 3 A.M. I awake out of a deep sleep and begin, for no apparent reason, to contemplate any number of weighty topics. I ponder how to raise my child, the fate of my limited investments in the stock market, my career, the future of our country. Or God. A few thoughts along these lines are enough to banish sleep for hours. But just when my fretting reaches a crescendo, I reach over to my wife and place my hand on whichever part of her is closest. My world stops spinning out of control. My heart slows. I drift off to sleep.

Touch. Glorious touch! Scientists have found that touch can reduce tension, elevate mood, enhance self-esteem, and perhaps even strengthen the immune system. Granted, not all touch in marriage is welcome. At certain moments, and for certain people, it can be seen as a demand or

I loved you in the morning,
our kisses deep and warm,
your hair upon the pillow
like a sleepy, golden storm.

Leonard (Norman) Cohen

even a rebuff. But much of the time, touching between couples can actually be more emotionally potent than the sex act itself. So during your pillow talk tonight, stay in touch with your partner—literally.

Before You Fall Asleep

Talk about how and when you most like to be touched by your partner—in and out of bed. Discuss the messages, both good and bad, you sometimes send each other through touch. In other words, take a moment to refine your communication of touch.

A Verse to Sleep On

SO HUSBANDS OUGHT TO LOVE THEIR OWN WIVES AS THEIR OWN BODIES; HE WHO LOVES HIS WIFE LOVES HIMSELF (EPHESIANS 5:28).

A Good Night Prayer

Lord, we appreciate the powerful effects of touch. You hardwired us to enjoy this great gift and we thank You for it. Remind us of how meaningful this is, especially when words fail us. Amen.

Scientists have found that touch can reduce tension, elevate mood, enhance self-esteem, and perhaps even strengthen the immune system.

You Snooze You Lose, Except in Bed

LEONARDO DA VINCI WOULD BITE HIS TONGUE TO FEND OFF FATIGUE AND WOULD SLEEP ONLY FIFTEEN MINUTES EVERY FOUR HOURS—A GRAND TOTAL OF AN HOUR-AND-A-HALF PER DAY. The painter Salvador Dali napped sitting with a spoon in his hand and a tin plate at his feet so that the moment he was overtaken by deep slumber, the spoon would fall, clatter, and awaken him refreshed. Charles Lindbergh spoke with ghosts over the Atlantic in order to make his historic thirty-three-hour solo flight between New York and Paris.

So, do you think these accomplished men found the secret to wringing more life out of life? Do you share their goal to become a productive insomniac? Whether you do or don't, you might be interested in a recent finding on sleep.

Cornell psychology professor James Maas is among a growing number of sleep experts who worry that

The amount of sleep required by the average person is about an hour more.

Anonymous

most of us spend our days desperately in need of a good night's sleep. The average length of sleep in this country right now is less than seven hours, and a third of us are getting six or less. Maas has written a book, *Power Sleep*, in which he claims sleep deprivation has become a crisis. And here's how he says you can tell if you're sleep deprived: If you need an alarm clock to wake up; if you fall asleep during the day, like in a boring meeting; and if you fall asleep immediately after your head hits the pillow.

Also, researchers from the Army and the National Institutes of Health have, actually seen images of the human brain at different stages of sleep, including when the brain hasn't had enough sleep. Their study shows that sleep deprivation most affects the region of your brain that mediates the highest order mental processes, the ability to think ahead, to plan, to creatively problem solve.

Even if your body feels rested, your brain may not. And everything suffers—your memory, your creativity, your ability to plan and solve problems. So take note and be sure your brain, not just your body, is wide awake tomorrow.

Before You Fall Asleep

Rate your restfulness on a scale of one to ten. What can you do, in specific terms, to help each other get the rest you need? Would it help to have the room darker, quieter, share the late-night child care, or what? Help each other sleep well.

A Verse to Sleep On

I WILL BOTH LIE DOWN IN PEACE, AND SLEEP; FOR YOU ALONE, O LORD, MAKE ME DWELL IN SAFETY (PSALM 4:8).

A Good Night Prayer

God, when modern science reveals a tiny glimpse into the mystery of Your creation help us to be good stewards of it. Help us not to fight the natural laws You have put in place in our bodies. Give us a restful sleep so that this body You have created can do the restorative work You've created it to do. Amen.

Sleep deprivation most affects the region of your brain that mediates the highest order mental processes, the ability to think ahead, to plan, to creatively problem solve. So even if your body feels rested, your brain may not.

Sleep is the golden chain that ties health and our bodies together.

THOMAS DEKKER

Beauty Sleep for the Soul

IT'S 7:30 A.M. WHEN A KNOCK ON THE DOOR ROUSTS MISS UNIVERSE FROM A DEEP SLUMBER. The 20-year-old native of Botswana groggily rises, looking more like Miss Bad Hair. "Phone for you," says the manager, apologetically. At 7:45 in the next bedroom, the alarm buzzes—the cue for 22-year-old Miss USA to shuffle down the hall and plug in her curlers before flopping back into bed.

It could be reveille in any dorm—except these roommates really do need their beauty sleep. And truth is, we all do. A decent night's sleep is important because while you're sleeping, your cells' renewal process is working at its hardest. Nighttime is when damaged skin cells repair themselves and recoup their energy to protect the skin again the following day. That's why many women apply night creams jam-packed with goodies for optimum nourishment of the nocturnal skin. To get the maximum benefit from those hardworking cells, and look your best, you first have to be assured of a good night's sleep.

Tonight, however, we want you both to consider a different kind of "beauty sleep." This kind requires no expensive creams or lotions. We're talking about beauty sleep that focuses on your character—how beautiful you are on the inside.

Here's your assignment. Focus your pillow talk tonight on what kind of "cream" you'd like to apply to your character if you could. After a night's sleep, maybe this lotion would help you become more patient with others, for example. Or maybe the beauty cream would make you more disciplined or goal-oriented. Perhaps it would help you delay gratification or increase your level of kindness or generosity. Maybe your cream would give you more empathy and understanding to sooth conflicts.

As you are turning in tonight, be sure to get your beauty sleep, for your face, sure—but for your soul as well.

Before You Fall Asleep

Get specific about how you would like to have more of a healthy quality in your character by sun up. Talk about it with each other and take a moment to pray that God would begin to realize that quality within you.

A Verse to Sleep On

HE WHO DWELLS IN THE SHELTER OF THE MOST HIGH WILL
REST IN THE SHADOW OF THE ALMIGHTY (PSALM 91:1, NIV).

A Good Night Prayer

*God, as we sleep tonight help us be mindful of how
Your spirit can work within us. We've identified
some qualities we'd like to cultivate. Massage them
into our spirit this evening and help us to
consciously work on them throughout the day
tomorrow. Amen.* ☾

In the Morning

You prayed for personal growth last night. Now
it's time to pray about it again, then get up and
go live it!

Give me humility, in which
alone is rest, and deliver
me from pride, which is
the heaviest of burdens.

Thomas Merton

Report at Eleven

"I DIDN'T KNOW YOU AND GARY PLANNED A SKI TRIP FOR NEXT MONTH," LESLIE SAID AS I HUNG UP THE PHONE WITH MY FRIEND GARY.

"Sure you did," I responded. "You were at dinner that night when I told him it would be great to meet in Colorado this winter. Don't you remember?"

"I remember being at dinner with you and Gary, but I don't recall any plans for a ski trip."

Ever had one of those conversations? Or how about this one:

"What do you mean we're going to the Campbells' tomorrow night? You never told me about this."

"Sure I did. Suzy and I planned this ages ago."

Or how about this:

"Honey, did I hear you telling your dad on the phone that you landed an important contract yesterday at work?"

"Yes, I meant to tell you about that . . ."

It seems most couples, traveling at the speed of life, don't always have a chance to update each other on the happenings of their lives. We move so quickly that when we get home and begin to wind down, our minds shift into neutral.

One of the best ways to counter this experience is with a simple question we've been asking each other for years, often at day's end as we are crawling into bed: "What are the headlines of your life I didn't read today?" We both know what that means. It's our way of asking to be brought up to speed with anything we don't know about each other and our days.

Give it a try. There's no need to be out of the know. And a little late night pillow talk about what's going on in your life is always worthwhile.

Before You Fall Asleep

Try this. Tell your partner the one thing you are most excited about this week. Then tell about the one thing that worries you most or that weighs heaviest on your heart.

A Verse to Sleep On

THE LIPS OF THE RIGHTEOUS FEED MANY, BUT FOOLS DIE FOR LACK OF WISDOM (PROVERBS 10:21).

A Good Night Prayer

Lord, slow us down and help us to give our souls time to catch up. It's so tempting to move through life quickly, never taking time to get caught up with each other and ourselves. Help us, right now, to relax and stay in tune. Amen. ℭ

A Real Good, Good Night Kiss

AT A CHURCH NEAR OUR HOME IN SEATTLE, A
JAPANESE COUPLE, RECENT ARRIVALS IN THE UNITED
STATES, WERE GETTING MARRIED. Despite their
limited exposure to Western customs, the American-
style wedding went well. But when the minister
invited the couple to kiss, nothing happened.
Surprised, the minister turned to the bride and said,
"How about a little kiss?" Not wanting to offend,
she shyly leaned forward and kissed the minister!

She's not the first bride to be confused by kissing. A
kiss can mean different things at different times—
good morning, goodbye, I missed you, I'm sorry, I
love you, I'm in the mood, and so on. But perhaps

the sweetest of all kisses is the good night kiss that says I'm going to be missing you even while I sleep. Remember when you were dating each other and how difficult it was to say good night after a date? You'd say good night countless times with just as many kisses.

When was the last time you shared such a genuine good night kiss? One of our favorite verses in Proverbs (24:26, NIV) says: "An honest answer is like a kiss on the lips." Solomon, in all his wisdom, equaled a kiss on the lips to an honest answer. When we are kissing our spouse on the lips, especially as a way to say good night, we are conveying our honest feelings. It's a kind of lover's shorthand to the questions we rarely articulate but deeply feel at day's end: Do you still love me, in spite of all the mistakes I made today?

The sound of a kiss is not so loud as that of a cannon, but its echo lasts a great deal longer.

Oliver Wendell Holmes

Do you still want to be with me when I burn the toast, leave my clothes on the floor, and do all the rest? A good night kiss on the lips is a way of honestly answering in the affirmative these unspoken questions.

So tonight, give it some consideration. Don't take it for granted. Don't kiss flippantly. Give one another a real good, good night kiss and then enjoy the sweet slumber of a couple whose love is as honest as their hearts.

Before You Fall Asleep

Recall the first time the two of you kissed. What was going through your minds? Now, as a married couple, when and how do you like to be kissed by your spouse?

A Verse to Sleep On

AN HONEST ANSWER IS LIKE A KISS ON THE LIPS
(PROVERBS 24:26, NIV).

A Good Night Prayer

Lord, there are few things we treasure more than the loving expression of a tender kiss. Thanks for this gift. Help us to communicate our honest love with a kiss more often. And help us never to take these kisses for granted. Amen.

Give one another a real good, good night kiss and then enjoy the sweet slumber of a couple whose love is as honest as their hearts

Giving Satin Sheets a Whirl

SHINY. SMOOTH. LUSTROUS. EVEN THE WORDS DESCRIBING THEM SOUND SENSUAL. Satin sheets evoke the epitome of a bed that is ready for lovemaking. To slide between these silky sheets and cozy up to your husband or wife is bound to get most couples in the mood. Truth be told, however, whether you sleep on satin, cotton, flannel, or linen, the kind of sheets on your bed say little about your love life. Far more telling is the status of your relationship outside the bedroom.

While biology, especially the neurochemistry that determines each person's hormonal levels, is a significant factor in sexual motivation, it has long been established that couples who are intentional about their sex lives enjoy more fulfillment between the sheets. What does this mean? First, these couples aren't afraid to schedule times of physical intimacy. While this might sound like it takes all the spontaneity out of it, you won't hear these couples complaining. Second, these couples talk to each other about what they like and don't like when it comes to sex. And they respect each other's desires.

The point is that if your sex life isn't all you want it to be, you can do more than purchase an expensive set of satin sheets. As a married couple you have the opportunity to enjoy something wonderful.

Married people, by the way, have better sex lives than single people. Get this: Married people are about twice as likely as unmarried people to make love at least two or three times a week. And that's not all: Married sex is more fun. Forty-eight percent of husbands say sex with their partners is extremely satisfying, compared to just thirty-seven percent of cohabiting men.

So as you slip between the sheets tonight—satin or not—take a moment to inventory your sex life and, if need be, get intentional about how to make it better.

Before You Fall Asleep

Start thinking about one thing you can change that would improve your lovemaking. Then make a date for sometime in the next week to explore each other's ideas.

A Verse to Sleep On

THEN THE RIB WHICH THE LORD GOD HAD TAKEN FROM MAN HE MADE INTO A WOMAN, AND HE BROUGHT HER TO THE MAN. AND ADAM SAID: "THIS IS NOW BONE OF MY BONES AND FLESH OF MY FLESH; SHE SHALL BE CALLED WOMAN, BECAUSE SHE WAS TAKEN OUT OF MAN." THEREFORE A MAN SHALL LEAVE HIS FATHER AND MOTHER AND BE JOINED TO HIS WIFE, AND THEY SHALL BECOME ONE FLESH. AND THEY WERE BOTH NAKED, THE MAN AND HIS WIFE, AND WERE NOT ASHAMED (GENESIS 2:22-25).

A Good Night Prayer

Father, the mysteries, wonders, and pleasures of sex in marriage are a divine gift and we celebrate that. Thank You for blessing us with such intense enjoyment as husband and wife. Dwell in our marriage and enhance our oneness. Amen. ℂ

A Good Eight Hours?
Get Serious!

I (LESLIE) WAS HAVING A SLEEPLESS NIGHT—AN
EVENING CUP OF COFFEE, MY ILL HUSBAND'S
COUGHING AND RESTLESSNESS, AND DETAILS ABOUT
AN UPCOMING TRIP WERE KEEPING ME HOPELESSLY
AWAKE. Even after I slipped into the guest bedroom,
I still had trouble. Finally, at 3:15 A.M., I crawled
back into my own bed, next to a now half-awake
husband. "Can I do anything to help you sleep?" he
whispered with a groggy voice.

I couldn't believe it. Les was having a miserable night
himself and still wanted to know if he could do anything
to help me sleep better. I suppose I would have offered
the same thing. And my guess is you would also show
concern for your spouse. Why? Because we all know
how valuable a good night's sleep is.

We all need sleep. It's not a luxury. People from
every part of the world, hippos in the jungle, fish in
aquariums—they all sleep! Sleep is as important as
breathing or eating. In fact, people can survive longer

O sleep! O gentle sleep!

Nature's soft nurse

WILLIAM SHAKESPEARE

As you help each other become more rested, you and your relationship will operate at the optimum level.

without food than they can without sleep. Without adequate sleep our bodies pay a serious price. We become sluggish in our thinking. Irrational. Irritable. Our reaction times slow down. We become more vulnerable to illness. We even age more quickly and gain weight more easily. Experts tell us we require about eight hours to function at our best. Yet one-third of adults report they normally sleep less than six-and-a-half hours a night. And even those hours are not always restful.

So why don't the two of you have some pillow talk tonight about how you can help each other become better sleepers. It may sound strange, but as you help each other become more rested, you and your relationship will operate at the optimum level. Think of all the needless conflicts you can avoid. Here are a few suggestions to get you started: getting to bed consistently at the same time each night, exercising at some point in the day, not snacking late at night, giving each other a gentle back rub before dozing off, and so on. The point is to get serious about your sleep and discuss specific ways that each of you can help the other sleep better—starting tonight. Your marriage will thank you later.

Before You Fall Asleep

Ideally, how many hours a night would you like
to sleep? What helps you sleep at your optimum?
What is your ideal way of being awoken in the
morning? What can you do to make your bedroom
a better place for the two of you to sleep?

A Verse to Sleep On

BY DAY THE LORD DIRECTS HIS LOVE, AT NIGHT HIS SONG IS
WITH ME—A PRAYER TO THE GOD OF MY LIFE (PSALM 42:8, NIV).

A Good Night Prayer

*Father, we often take sleep for granted but You
built it into our lives and created us to be reenergized
by it. Help us to be good stewards of our sleep and
give it the attention it deserves. And tonight as we
fall asleep we want to thank You for this restorative
gift that makes our waking hours all the more
valuable. Amen.* ℭ

In the Morning

How did you sleep last night? How did you wake up?

HUSBAND

WIFE

Talking in Your Sleep?
You Can Do Better Than That

MARYELLA WORE A WOOL JACKET TO WORK ONE DAY, AND ON HER WAY HOME SHE DECIDED TO GET THE CAR WASHED. Because it had warmed up outside, she slipped her jacket off while she waited for the car to be cleaned. The next morning, her jacket was nowhere to be found. *Maybe I left it at the car wash*, she wondered as she called the number. "Did I leave a burgundy blazer there yesterday?" she asked the young man who answered. A minute later he returned from checking. "I'm sorry, Ma'am. There's no burgundy Blazer here, just a gray Bronco."

This is just another example of how easy it is to miscommunicate. It happens all the time, especially in marriage. Men and women, as has been pointed out in numerous best-sellers, sometimes communicate like they are from different planets. A survey of more than 1,000 married couples reported in *U.S. News and World Report* found that we don't even talk about the same things. The leading discussion subject for men is news events (talked about in the previous week by 71 percent of respondents), followed by work (68 percent). Women, on the other hand, talked about food (76 percent) and health (72 percent). Men were far more likely to have talked about sports (65 percent to women's 42 percent); women were more likely to have discussed personal problems (52 percent to men's 40 percent).

Whatever the topic, however, we share one thing in common. Husbands and wives depend on communication to keep their relationship running. It is the lifeblood of every marriage. Couples who can't communicate soon fall apart. So as you are winding down this evening and crawling into bed, consider how well you are doing at this important task. How well do you communicate as a couple? "The road to the heart," wrote Voltaire, "is the ear." Are you good listeners even when the topic isn't one of your favorites? Carefully listening to your partner—throughout the day and deep into the night—is the quickest path to intimacy.

Before You Fall Asleep

Rate how well you communicate as a couple on a scale of one to ten and compare your answers. What is one aspect of communication that you each could improve beginning tomorrow?

A Verse to Sleep On

DO NOT LET ANY UNWHOLESOME TALK COME OUT OF YOUR MOUTHS, BUT ONLY WHAT IS HELPFUL FOR BUILDING OTHERS UP ACCORDING TO THEIR NEEDS, THAT IT MAY BENEFIT THOSE WHO LISTEN (EPHESIANS 4:29, NIV).

A Good Night Prayer

Lord, as we fall asleep tonight we ask that You create in us the capacity to listen to each other as You listen to us. Amen. ☾

The woods are lovely, dark and deep.

But I have promises to keep,

And miles to go before I sleep

And miles to go before I sleep.

ROBERT FROST

Goodnight Moon . . . Again

"IN THE GREAT GREEN ROOM THERE WAS A TELEPHONE AND A RED BALLOON AND A PICTURE OF A COW JUMPING OVER THE MOON." So begins the first line of a children's book we have been reading nearly nightly for the past several months. Our little guy, John, is three years old and can barely put his head on the pillow of his "big boy bed" without one of us reading this story narrated by a pajama clad bunny. And we aren't the only parents who have this one memorized.

Margaret Wise Brown published the now-classic children's story *Goodnight Moon* in 1947. It sells better today than it did back then, and it has created a

nightly ritual for legions of little ones who have to say good night to the red balloon and the moon before turning in.

Reading this story night after night got us to thinking about our own rituals. On any given evening at our house, about the time our local nightly news begins to air, you're likely to find both of us perusing the cereal boxes lined up in our kitchen pantry. Bran Flakes or Frosted? Shredded Wheat or Special K? It's a scene that has occurred countless times over the course of nearly two decades of marriage. We never planned this nightly ritual; it just happened. And now it's reflexive, a habit. Whoever gets there first typically sets out a bowl and spoon for the other. We do it by instinct and this seemingly inconsequential

act at the end of our day has become one of the many panels in the quilt of behaviors we've sewn together as a couple.

Every husband and wife, knowingly or not, have dozens of deeds similar to this that they do out of habit—some more helpful to the relationship than others. Tonight, before you fall asleep consider your rituals, seemingly insignificant or not, and how they fortify your relationship. Rituals have a way of grounding us. They provide security and comfort. So give them a little attention to keep them going or to cultivate a new one.

Before You Fall Asleep

What is your favorite daily or weekly ritual as a couple? What does it do for you and your marriage? And what new daily, weekly, or even yearly ritual might you like to incorporate into your life together?

A Verse to Sleep On

I LAY DOWN AND SLEPT; I AWOKE, FOR THE LORD SUSTAINED ME (PSALM 3:5).

A Good Night Prayer

Father, in this unstable world we desperately need the security of Your unchanging spirit. You are the same yesterday, today, and forever. Thank You for your abiding love. Thank You for Your unfailing faithfulness. Amen.

Now cracks a noble heart. Good night sweet prince: And flights of angels sing thee to thy rest!

William Shakespeare

The Princess and the Pea, It's a Good Thing

ONCE UPON A TIME THERE WAS A PRINCE WHO WANTED TO MARRY A PRINCESS. He traveled all over the world to find a real princess, but nowhere could he get what he wanted. One evening a princess knocked at the city gate seeking shelter. To find out if she was a real princess, the queen devised a plan. She took all the bedding off the bedstead, and laid a pea on the bottom; then she took twenty mattresses and laid them on the pea. In the morning the princess was asked how she had slept, and the sensitive young woman mentioned she'd felt an uncomfortable little lump. The prince now knew he had a real princess.

When Hans Christian Anderson wrote that story in 1835 he was simply entertaining children. But all these years later, we think there is a lesson in it for every married couple. That is, that a true "prince" or "princess" notices the little things, especially the little things that can make a big difference. A "real" husband or wife, for example, recognizes when their spouse needs help bringing in the groceries. Or when their spouse is feeling overwhelmed by something at work and could use a tender back rub. In other words, a sensitive and responsive spouse is on the lookout for ways to be supportive.

This person is not only supportive, however, they recognize the positive little things that go unnoticed by most. A "real" husband or wife, for example, recognizes when their spouse takes out the trash and they say thanks. Like the princess and the pea, they notice when the bed has been freshly made with clean sheets or when their partner picked up the coat left hanging over the back of a chair. They notice when their beloved filled the car with gas and when they took care to make the yard look nice.

Bottom line, we strengthen our marriage whenever we take time to lend a hand and whenever we notice and appreciate the little things our partner does to help us out. So before you say your good nights, take a moment to say thanks for something little you noticed today.

Before You Fall Asleep

What little thing did your partner do or say today that you didn't have a chance to tell him or her how much you appreciated it?

A Verse to Sleep On

FINALLY, BRETHREN, WHATEVER THINGS ARE TRUE, WHATEVER THINGS ARE NOBLE, WHATEVER THINGS ARE JUST, WHATEVER THINGS ARE PURE, WHATEVER THINGS ARE LOVELY, WHATEVER THINGS ARE OF GOOD REPORT, IF THERE IS ANY VIRTUE AND IF THERE IS ANYTHING PRAISEWORTHY—MEDITATE ON THESE THINGS (PHILIPPIANS 4:8).

A Good Night Prayer

Lord, make us more sensitive to the little things we can do to be a better spouse. Help us to be on the lookout for ways to lend a hand to each other. And help us to take note of the little things our partner does that we too often take for granted. Lord, make us mindful of all the little blessings You shower on us each day. Amen.

Finding the Prize Under Your Pillow

A PROMOTION BY H&R BLOCK INC. OFFERED WALK-IN CUSTOMERS A CHANCE TO WIN A DRAWING FOR A MILLION DOLLARS. Glen and Gloria Sims of New Jersey won the drawing, but they refused to believe it when an H&R Block representative phoned them with the good news. After additional contacts by both mail and phone, the Sims still thought it was all just a scam, and usually hung up the phone or trashed the special notices.

Some weeks later, H&R Block called one more time to let the Sims know the deadline for accepting the million-dollar prize was nearing and that the story of their refusal to accept the prize would appear on an upcoming NBC *Today* show. At that point, Mr. Sims decided to investigate further. A few days later he appeared on the *Today* show to tell America that he and his wife had finally gone to H&R Block to claim the million-dollar prize.

The future belongs to those who believe in the beauty of their dreams.

ELEANOR ROOSEVELT

Amazing, isn't it? A million-dollar prize waiting for them to claim, but they were skeptical. Truth is, any of us could have done the same thing. If you've been around long enough you know how easy it can be to be snookered by a sales gimmick. And if you've been married long enough, sadly, you may have fallen into the same trap with your spouse.

Knowingly or not, we sometimes put our partner in a box. *He's been like that for years*, we say, *so he'll never change.* But he or she can and will make positive changes, if you let it happen. If you refuse to see something good, small increments of improvement in some area, you make the change impossible. It's like not claiming a million-dollar prize when it's there for the asking. So quit rolling your eyes and set aside your skepticism to discover the good changes that may be taking place right beside you. If you don't believe in your spouse and cultivate confidence in his or her ability to grow, you will be missing out on a tremendous treasure.

Before You Fall Asleep

Talk to your spouse about what you would like to change in your own character. It may be a bad habit (with money or health issues) or a bad attitude (about parenting or in-laws). As each of you shares this, express, in turn, your optimism and confidence about him or her being able to make a positive change.

A Verse to Sleep On

I WILL PRAISE THE LORD, WHO COUNSELS ME; EVEN AT NIGHT MY HEART INSTRUCTS ME (PSALM 16:7, NIV).

A Good Night Prayer

Lord, don't allow skepticism to play a part in our marriage. Infuse us with confidence in each other tonight. As we sleep, bolster our minds with images of the goodness in each other. ☾

A ruffled mind makes a restless pillow.

Charlotte Bronte

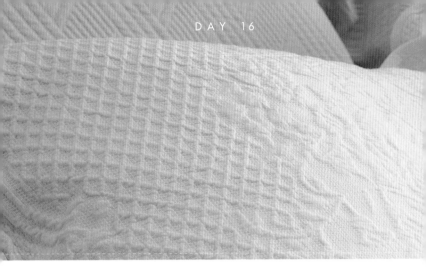

Your Side of the Bed or Mine?

OKAY, LADIES, THIS ONE'S FOR YOU. SCIENCE HAS FINALLY CONFIRMED WHAT YOU'VE LONG KNOWN: YOUR HUSBAND WHO SNORES, TOSSES, AND TURNS AT NIGHT CAN SIGNIFICANTLY COMPROMISE YOUR OWN SLEEP. A study at the Mayo Clinic in Rochester, Minnesota, found that when men who have sleep apnea (in which breathing stops periodically during sleep that is commonly associated with snoring) wore a device that helped them breathe at night, the continuity of their wives' sleep improved thirteen percent. The women got the equivalent of an extra sixty-two minutes of shut-eye a night.

But that's not all. When researchers at Loughborough

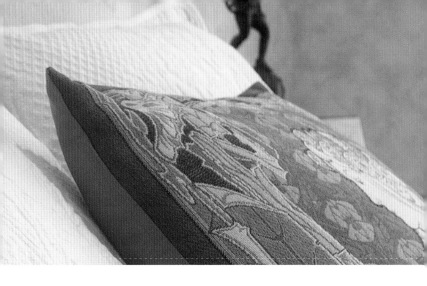

University in England kept track of how forty-six couples moved their bodies as they slept, they found that women were disturbed by their partner's movements more frequently than men were.

We're not trying to start a fight here, but if you're like the typical couple and wanting to improve your quality of sleep, we want you to be aware of a few coping strategies for both of you during your pillow talk tonight. First off, experts say you can aim for better snooze control by encouraging your spouse to avoid alcohol, caffeine, heavy meals, and exercise within a few hours of bedtime. These preventive measures may help your spouse sleep more soundly and move around less, which means you'll do the same. And if you are a snorer, sleep on your side instead of your

back to reduce your snore potential.

Let's face it, men and women are different—even how we sleep. Husbands and wives survive and thrive based on how well we flex, cope, and care for one another in the midst of our differences. At times that can be trying, but it's precisely what builds a better marriage, especially in the bedroom.

Before You Fall Asleep

We've identified a typical difference between the sexes at bedtime. Why don't you identify a difference you have worked out in another part of your relationship? As you recognize how well you compromised in one area you will have more energy to make healthy changes in others.

A Verse to Sleep On

AND THE PEACE OF GOD, WHICH SURPASSES ALL UNDER-
STANDING, WILL GUARD YOUR HEARTS AND MINDS THROUGH
CHRIST JESUS (PHILIPPIANS 4:7).

A Good Night Prayer

*God, we know You have created us differently
and that sometimes makes for a challenge. But
we also know our differences are what make life
interesting. So help us celebrate these differences
as best we can and learn to compromise on both
sides as much as possible. Amen.*

Finish each day before
you begin the next, and
interpose a solid wall of
sleep between the two.
This you cannot do without
temperance.

Ralph Waldo Emerson

Turning Down the Covers of Your Soul

ONE OF ENGLAND'S MAJOR NEWSPAPERS, *THE GUARDIAN*, CARRIES A DAILY CONFESSIONAL COLUMN CALLED "CORRECTIONS AND AMPLIFICATIONS." Edited by Ian Mayes, the column breaks the stodgy English tradition of rarely admitting error.

Sometimes done with humor at the paper's own expense, the column averages about five items per day. Typos range from simple misspellings to substituting "having insight" for "having incited." Mayes sensed that more people read the correction than read the original story. And he was right. He published a best selling book with a compendium of his favorite mishaps.

If a newspaper has learned that confession enlarges readership rather than turning people away, perhaps there is a lesson for husbands and wives here, too. Neither newspapers nor spouses can avoid making mistakes. But admitting and taking responsibility for them is particularly vital to couples.

So tonight, as you turn down the covers of your bed, why don't you take a moment to turn down the covers of your soul. Just a bit. Enough to let your spouse know you're human. Confess your foibles as a husband or wife. What "corrections and amplifications" on your part of the marriage today would you like to express? Perhaps you regret the comment you made about dinner tonight. Maybe you wish you had handled a discipline issue with the kids differently. Or maybe you wish you would have affirmed your partner at a certain point in the evening for how he or she handled a tough spot at work.

No one is perfect. We all make mistakes. But differences emerge, in ourselves and our marriage, when we own up to our mistakes and do our best to correct them. Try it. You'll sleep more soundly tonight.

Before You Fall Asleep

What little correction can you confess tonight? Review your day and highlight one thing you wish you would have handled differently—especially as it pertains to your marriage. The very act of talking about it will help you do better next time.

A Verse to Sleep On

HE WHO COVERS HIS SINS WILL NOT PROSPER, BUT WHOEVER CONFESSES AND FORSAKES THEM WILL HAVE MERCY (PROVERBS 28:13).

A Good Night Prayer

Father, we already know that confession is good for the soul. So give us the courage to do this more often. Help us take responsibility for the things we can correct. It's tough to do this at times and we need Your help. Amen. ℭ

Hurry Up and Sleep!

IN HIS BOOK *STRESS FRACTURES*, CHARLES SWINDOLL WRITES ABOUT A TIME WHEN HE WAS IN THE UNDERTOW OF TOO MANY COMMITMENTS IN TOO FEW DAYS. Before long, the whole Swindoll family was becoming impacted by Chuck's hurry-up style and it was becoming unbearable. "I distinctly recall after supper one evening the words of our younger daughter, Colleen." She wanted to tell her father about something important that had happened to her at school that day. She hurriedly began, "Daddy-I-wanna-tell-you-somethin'-and-I'll-tell-you-really-fast." Suddenly realizing her frustration, Chuck answered, "Honey, you can tell me . . . and you don't have to tell me really fast. Say it slowly."

"I'll never forget her answer," he said: "Then listen slowly."

Have you ever been infected with hurry sickness? I know we have. And most other couples we know have combated it as well. That's one of the reasons pillow talk is so important. Bedtime forces us to slow

down. Even as we get under the cover we begin to breathe more deeply and slowly. Our body temperature drops slightly, and our heart rate and blood pressure go down. Muscles relax. Our metabolic rate slows down, too. Falling asleep is nature's way of helping us conserve energy and refuel our tanks.

So as you hit the hay tonight, take a moment to savor the change in your pace. Notice your body's desire to lean into this antidote to stress and hurry. Talk to each other about your busy day and then dream a bit about scheduling some time to downshift your lifestyle pace. This is a perfect topic for pillow talk. Considering what you can do to live a more balanced life is most productive when you are relaxing. Making specific plans and working on schedules is better left to the more productive times of the day, but bedtime is a good moment to explore how you might like to change the pace of your life.

Before You Fall Asleep

Identify something specific you can change in your schedule tomorrow to slow it down just a bit. Talk about what you like and dislike about being busy.

A Verse to Sleep On

IN VAIN YOU RISE EARLY AND STAY UP LATE, TOILING FOR FOOD TO EAT—FOR HE GRANTS SLEEP TO THOSE HE LOVES (PSALM 127:2, NIV).

A Good Night Prayer

Father, help each of us to seize our days. Don't allow us to rush through our weeks and wonder what happened. Slow us down. We call on You to give us perspective so that we spend our time on the things that matter most. Amen. ℂ

In the Morning

Take a deep breath. Tell yourself it's OK to slow down sometimes. How can you savor today more?

HUSBAND

_____

_____

_____

WIFE

_____

_____

_____

Bedtime is a good moment to explore how you might like to change the pace of your life.

Counting Blessings, Not Sheep

A FRIEND OF OURS TOLD US ABOUT HER THREE-YEAR-OLD SON, JUSTIN, AND HIS CREATIVE TACTICS FOR STAYING AWAKE PAST HIS BEDTIME. On one particular night, the bedtime rituals had extended longer than the allotted time, and Justin's requests had gone beyond the second drink of water and more stories. But our friend and her husband were soon caught off guard when Justin yelled from his room, "Can three people fit in a big bed?" When they answered yes, he said, "Okay, I'll be right over."

Children can be our biggest cause of annoyance and yet our greatest source of blessing. If you have little ones at your home, like we do, you know just what we mean. But whether you have children or not, you know how easy it is to focus on our annoyances, whatever they might be, rather than our blessings. That's why we love the suggestion somebody recently gave us for falling asleep. Instead of counting sheep, they suggested counting your blessings. Talk about

sweet dreams! Isn't that a great idea? We've found it to be a helpful bedtime practice whether it's designed to prevent insomnia or not.

So as you slide between the sheets tonight, take a moment to note the things you are grateful for. Count your blessings. In fact, just consider the last forty-eight hours and what you've encountered in your life that you've probably taken for granted. Share with your spouse, in specific terms, what these blessings might be. Perhaps you're grateful for living in a free country, having mind-boggling technology, enjoying the simple beauty of your garden, listening to beautiful music, or relishing a home cooked meal. Take a moment to note as many blessings as you can from your past two days. This will go a long way in helping you enjoy another blessing—a good night's rest.

Before You Fall Asleep

What is one specific way that you can be a blessing to your partner tomorrow? Share with each other what you might be able to do to make each other's days easier.

A Verse to Sleep On

LET MY MOUTH BE FILLED WITH YOUR PRAISE AND WITH YOUR GLORY ALL THE DAY (PSALM 71:8).

A Good Night Prayer

Father, we have so much to be grateful for. And tonight, as we count our blessings, we acknowledge that You have brought these good things to us. We are humbled by Your goodness. Help us to fill every hour of our day tomorrow with appreciation for Your gifts.

Have courage for the great sorrows of life and patience for the small ones; and when you have laboriously accomplished your daily task, go to sleep in peace. God is awake.

Victor Hugo

The Self-Inflating Mattress Syndrome

HANNAH, A CHURCH ORGANIST FOR MANY YEARS, HAD TAKEN TO FALLING ASLEEP DURING THE SERMON. As she was loved by all, this fault was easily overlooked. Besides, the position of the organ at the end of the platform kept her pretty much away from the congregation's normal line of vision.

One Sunday as the sermon was building to its height, the minister swung his arm forcefully and cried: "Look to the east!" The congregation, following his gesture, gasped and then chuckled softly. There sat Hannah, head back and mouth open, sleeping the sleep of the innocent. The minister regained his composure and concluded his message with equal poise. Hannah awoke at her usual time and played the closing hymn, temporarily unaware of what had happened.

It may have been different circumstances, but we've all been in Hannah's shoes. We've all suffered a humiliating experience that brought us down a notch or two. And that's not a bad thing.

Just like a self-inflating mattress becomes puffed up with nothing but air, we can puff ourselves up with hollow pride. You know the syndrome. You've seen it in others and, if you're honest, you've seen it in yourself. We can become so impressed with whom we think we are that we lose all sight of our humility. And humility is a key ingredient to any healthy relationship, especially marriage. William Gurnall said, "Humility is the necessary veil to all other graces." Without humility, it's nearly impossible to engender kindness and warmth with our spouse.

So before you fall asleep tonight, check your unhealthy pride quotient. Consider what the famous Victorian preacher Charles Spurgeon said: "Humility is to make a right assessment of oneself." As a married couple, you have a built-in way for doing just that. You can invite feedback, although it takes some courage, to help you honestly assess how you're doing with pride. But by all means, be gentle with each other.

Before You Fall Asleep

Ask your spouse to help you identify one area in your life where it wouldn't hurt to have a bit more humility. Listen to his or her feedback without being defensive. The goal is to help, not hurt, one another.

A Verse to Sleep On

(JESUS) SAID, ASSUREDLY, I SAY TO YOU, UNLESS YOU ARE CONVERTED AND BECOME AS LITTLE CHILDREN, YOU WILL BY NO MEANS ENTER THE KINGDOM OF HEAVEN. THEREFORE WHOEVER HUMBLES HIMSELF AS THIS LITTLE CHILD IS THE GREATEST IN THE KINGDOM OF HEAVEN (MATTHEW 18:3-4).

A Good Night Prayer

Lord, pride is an easy stumbling block. Please help both of us to be mindful of how it interferes with our relationships—especially our marriage. Teach us to humble ourselves with each other instead of trying to get our own way. Amen. ©

Good night, good night! parting is such sweet sorrow,

That I shall say good night till it be morrow.

WILLIAM SHAKESPEARE

Not Another Day of Sleep Walking

DO YOU REMEMBER YOUR FIRST NIGHTTIME PRAYERS. If you were like countless other children, you prayed, "Now I lay me down to sleep . . ." Remember that? There's a line from that prayer that's worth reconsidering. In fact, it was our friend Tony Campolo that brought it to our attention.

Tony was taking a course in Chinese philosophy during his graduate education. The Buddhist monk who taught the course told him, "As a Christian, you teach your children to pray all wrong. You teach them to pray, 'If I should die before I wake.' It would be better if you taught them to pray, 'If I should wake before I die.'"

The monk went on to point out that most of the people he knew were half-awake when they ought to be asleep. But even worse, when they were awake, they were half-asleep. No one seemed to be totally alive. He's got a point, doesn't he?

Too often we meander through our days without purpose, without energy, and without life. We are like sleep walkers who hope to wake before we die. So before you turn the lights out tonight, consider how you can live tomorrow for all it's worth. How can you make your day count? What can you do to find meaning in each moment?

Here's a place to start: Identify what you really want. Maybe it's more time with your children. Maybe it's financial freedom. Maybe it's to complete a project

you've been postponing. The key is to identify what you want most from tomorrow. This is what will give you purpose and direction. We have a friend who puts it this way: Know what you ardently desire, sincerely believe in, vividly imagine, enthusiastically act on, and you will live each day for all it's worth. We couldn't agree more.

Before You Fall Asleep

Take a moment to discuss what would make tomorrow meaningful for you. Twenty-four hours from now, what would you like to look back on and say, that was time well spent?

A Verse to Sleep On

NOW FAITH IS THE SUBSTANCE OF THINGS HOPED FOR, THE EVIDENCE OF THINGS NOT SEEN (HEBREWS 11:1).

A Good Night Prayer

Lord, we confess that it's easy to wander into our days, mistaking business for meaningful activity. Protect us from sleep walking through our days. Help us seize each moment tomorrow by seeking what You want most from us. Amen. ℭ

In the Morning

How are you going to make life more meaningful today?

HUSBAND

WIFE

Know what you ardently desire, sincerely believe in, vividly imagine, enthusiastically act on, and you will live each day for all it's worth

The Best Rest Ever

BOSTON IS ONE OF OUR FAVORITE CITIES. LES GREW UP THERE. And each time we get back to "Bean Town" for a speaking engagement we try to do something different with our down time. One year we visited the Holocaust Memorial downtown where six pillars are inscribed with quotes and stories that speak of the cruelty and suffering in the camps. One story is about a girl named Ilse, a childhood friend of Gerda Weissman Klein who was like her only family in the forced-labor camp. Gerda remembers that one morning Ilse found a single raspberry somewhere in the camp. Ilse carried it all day long in a protected place in her pocket, and in the evening, her eyes shining with happiness, she presented it to her friend on a leaf. "Imagine a world," writes Gerda, "in which your entire possession is one raspberry, and you give it to your friend."

It's tough to imagine such a world, isn't it? In fact, it's tough to image the kind of brutality the adults,

My candle burns at both ends

It will not last the night;

But ah, my foes, and oh, my friends—

It gives a lovely light.

EDNA ST. VINCENT MILLAY

not to mention the children, suffered in Nazi death camps. But it's not tough to be inspired by such a gracious and happy act of kindness—a simple berry, treasured to present to a friend. We note Ilse's generosity tonight because it is a breathtaking example of the kind of generosity the two of you can offer each other in marriage. Imagine a marriage in which you offer your prized possession to your mate, whatever it might be. Maybe it's your time when you have a pile of work on your desk. Maybe it's your listening ear when you'd planned on watching the game. Maybe it's your presence when a friend has invited you to go shopping. Your simple yet spectacular gift may only be known to you. But when you give it, you will sleep a deep and peaceful sleep.

So before you doze off tonight, take a lesson from Ilse and consider your generosity quotient. Consider what it would do for your marriage, as well as your night's sleep, if you increased it a notch or two.

Before You Fall Asleep

What kind gesture can you offer each other tomorrow? What act of generosity might you give? Share your ideas with each other and see what tomorrow might bring.

A Verse to Sleep On

WHOEVER DESIRES TO BECOME GREAT AMONG YOU SHALL BE YOUR SERVANT. AND WHOEVER OF YOU DESIRES TO BE FIRST SHALL BE SLAVE OF ALL. FOR EVEN THE SON OF MAN DID NOT COME TO BE SERVED, BUT TO SERVE, AND TO GIVE HIS LIFE A RANSOM FOR MANY (MARK 10:43-45).

A Good Night Prayer

Lord, we are humbled by a little girl named Ilse. We can't begin to imagine what her world was like, and we thank You for sparing us such misery. But help us use her kind act, in the midst of all her suffering, as an inspiration to show extraordinary kindness to each other. And Father, we can't help but to be reminded of the extravagant gift of grace You offered us as Your children. Teach us, each day, to give the same generous grace to each other. Amen. ❦

Imagine a marriage in which you offer your prized possession to your mate.

Hot and Heavy Between the Sheets

ALTHOUGH THE TYPICAL RED-BLOODED AMERICAN MALE WOULD NEVER DREAM OF PUBLICLY ADMITTING HIS HUNGER TO BE HELD, HIS CRAVING TO BE CARESSED, AND HIS YEARNING TO BE MASSAGED, IT IS AS REAL FOR MEN AS IT IS FOR WOMEN. In private, one of men's biggest complaints is that the wives don't touch them enough or in the special ways they would like them to.

Okay, you might say as a wife, *but isn't the type of touching at issue here—those gentle caresses designed to arouse and seduce—exactly the kind of time-consuming foreplay that exasperates men, according to conventional wisdom? Don't men prefer to move straight toward the nearest orgasm they can find?* Well, not exactly. Most men report that they, like women, enjoy being aroused for a reasonably long period of time before intercourse. It's just that men lack the language, and the courage, to express specific physical needs, to ask for what they really want. Instead of working to improve the process of arousal, the goal-oriented male focuses on the prize at the end of the rainbow.

In a recent counseling session after taking a brief inventory about their sex life, a husband told me that he loves touching his wife. "She has the softest skin and it feels so good to caress her," he confessed, "but I wish she would do the same for me." It's not the first time I've heard that.

So tonight, set aside expectations and use your pillow talk to explore one of the most important things that happens in your bed: lovemaking and all that leads to it. Use this opportunity to bridge the communication gap, and uncover what your partner likes and dislikes about being touched in the preamble to your lovemaking.

Before You Fall Asleep

Recount an occasion where you felt in sync physically. And if that's a distant memory (as it is for many couples) think of what that would mean for you and discuss it. What makes you feel like your partner is in tune with your desires? How open, on a scale of one to ten, do you feel you can be with each other on this topic?

A Verse to Sleep On

THE WIFE DOES NOT HAVE AUTHORITY OVER HER OWN BODY, BUT THE HUSBAND DOES. AND LIKEWISE THE HUSBAND DOES NOT HAVE AUTHORITY OVER HIS OWN BODY, BUT THE WIFE DOES (1 CORINTHIANS 7:4).

A Good Night Prayer

Lord, the topic of sex can be intimidating. Yet we know You created our maleness and femaleness on purpose and have given us a gift of sexual pleasure beyond compare. Give us the courage to talk about it and to make this gift all that You want it to be. Amen.

Good Night Prayers

"I FEEL CLOSER TO YOU WHEN WE PRAY TOGETHER,"
LESLIE RECENTLY TOLD ME. "It's probably the most
intimate thing we do." And she's right. It's part of
God's desiring that we walk together with Him,
not in a formal or legalistic way, but in a way that
is genuine and natural. God longs to be part of
every marriage, and prayer is one of the best ways
we know of for inviting Him into yours.

But let's get real. Spiritual intimacy, while vital to a
healthy marriage, so often seems elusive. Leslie and
I are the first to admit that we don't do this as well
as we'd like. We're not the types to kneel beside the
bed each night or morning and hold hands while we
call on God together. We'd probably be better for it,
but more often than not, our prayers together (other
than at meal times) are spontaneous and often
unexpected. But recently, after establishing the nightly
ritual of tucking in our three-year old, we've discovered
how meaningful it is to say a brief prayer together
before falling asleep.

Genuine prayer together lowers our defenses and heightens our teamwork. It joins our sprits together.

Maybe you already do this. If so, you know the harmony it brings to your marriage. As Paul Tournier points out, praying together enriches a couple's home—even with our differing temperaments, ideas, and tastes. Genuine prayer together lowers our defenses and heightens our teamwork. It joins our sprits together. And by the way, for all you skeptics thinking that prayer is for uptight people who can barely mention the word "sex," researchers have found something that might surprise you: couples who pray together have better sex lives. Why? Well, when a couple's body, soul, and spirit are in harmony with one another and with their Creator, physical intimacy becomes reminiscent of Paradise, and love returns to Eden.

So say your prayers tonight and every night that you can. It just may be the most important thing you do all day.

Before You Fall Asleep

Take a moment for each of you to share a specific prayer request for your day tomorrow. In other words, what would you like your spouse to remember for you in prayer to make your tomorrow better? And what specific thanksgiving do you have for the day that's just ending?

A Verse to Sleep On

AND PRAY IN THE SPIRIT ON ALL OCCASIONS WITH ALL KINDS OF PRAYERS AND REQUESTS. WITH THIS IN MIND, BE ALERT AND ALWAYS KEEP ON PRAYING FOR ALL THE SAINTS (EPHESIANS 6:18, NIV).

A Good Night Prayer

Lord, there is an ancient marriage prayer we offer tonight: May we two live our lives so happily together that You, God, may enjoy our union of heart and spirit with each other. Amen. ℭ

In the Morning

What did you agree last night to pray about today? Later, ask your beloved how it helped knowing you were praying.

HUSBAND

WIFE

Sleeping on Air

A COUPLE OF YEARS AGO I HAD AN ABUNDANCE OF AIR MILES THAT WERE GOING TO EXPIRE IF I DIDN'T USE THEM. Short on time but not wanting to waste them, I asked my dad if he'd like to fly first class to Rome, Italy, with me for four days. "Here's the deal," I told him. "I'll pay for the travel if you pick up the hotel." (Seemed fair to me!) He jumped at the chance and we had a terrific trip. The only downside was flying first class.

Don't get me wrong, I'm not complaining. But that experience has made all my other air travel seem so shoddy. Instead of the airline food I'm accustomed to, they served elegant cuisine that seemed to have no end—a fresh fruit and cheese plate, then the salad, followed by hot soup, delicious breads, and a mouth-watering entrée. For dessert? Hot fudge sundaes! We couldn't believe it. To top it all off they brought out a gold foil box of chocolates to nibble on while we watched the movie we selected for our individual screens. After the feast, the real benefit of flying first class kicked in. Our chairs reclined. Not just a little—into a full bed with a privacy curtain that encircled it. It was like a mini apartment on the plane.

I haven't had that kind of flying experience since, but I confess that I could get used to it. To amend the old airline commercial a bit, "It's the only way to sleep while you fly."

As Leslie and I have been putting together this little book, I began thinking about how nice all the accoutrements and special attention in the first-class cabin were. But I've got another confession. They don't hold a candle to sleeping with my wife in our own bed. For me, it's one of the safest places on earth. Since we married in 1984, we've had countless conversations that brought us closer together—even after the lights went out.

Our warm feeling about these times is part of what motivated us to write this book. We hope you will enjoy the first-class feeling of sleeping with your soul mate, sharing pillow talk that's sweeter than any box of chocolates.

Before You Fall Asleep

What do you enjoy most about getting to share your bed with your partner? We all have our complaints about the temperature of the bedroom and the hogging of the blanket. But looking beyond these predicable complaints, what do you like best about your pillow talk?

A Verse to Sleep On

THE SLEEP OF A LABORING MAN IS SWEET, WHETHER HE EATS LITTLE OR MUCH; BUT THE ABUNDANCE OF THE RICH WILL NOT PERMIT HIM TO SLEEP (ECCLESIASTES 5:12).

A Good Night Prayer

Lord, thank You for the blessing of the marriage bed. What a great place to laugh, love, and talk. Help us never to take this safe place for granted and always enjoy the benefits of pillow talk. Amen. ❦

About the Authors

Drs. Les and Leslie Parrott are co-directors of the Center for Relationships Development at Seattle Pacific University (SPU), a groundbreaking program dedicated to teaching the basics of good relationships. Les Parrott is a professor of clinical psychology at SPU, and Leslie is a marriage and family therapist at SPU.

The Parrotts are authors of the Gold Medallion Award-winning *Saving Your Marriage Before It Starts*, *Becoming Soul Mates*, *When Bad Things Happen to Good Marriages*, *Proverbs for Couples*, and *Love Is*. They have been featured on *Oprah*, *CBS This Morning*, *CNN*, and *The View*, and in *USA Today* and the *New York Times*.

They are also frequent guest speakers and have written for a variety of magazines. The Parrotts serve as marriage ambassadors for the Oklahoma governor's ten-year Marriage Initiative (2000–2010). They live in Seattle, Washington, with their son, John.

Visit their website at www.RealRelationships.com.